Mystic's Musings

Mind
Is Your Business

Sadhguru

DIAMOND BOOKS

Mind Is Your Business (Mystic's Musings Series)

Sadhguru

Copyright ©2013 Isha Foundation

First Edition: March 2013

ISBN: 978-93-5083-360-5

Published by:

Diamond Pocket Books Pvt. Ltd.

X-30, Okhla Industrial Area, Phase-II

New Delhi – 110020 (INDIA)

Tel: 011-40712100, 40716600

Email: sales@dpb.in

Website: www.diamondbook.in

Contents

Introduction 5

1. The Circus of the Mind 7

2. The Garbage Bin 27

3. A Ladder to the Divine 41

Introduction

The mind seems to be a rather dynamic entity – its mysterious workings have cast a spell on scientists, spiritual seekers, and even poets and novelists. Mark Twain once jested, "I must have a prodigious amount of mind; it takes me as much as a week sometimes to make it up." Though we freely use such terms as "never mind" and "mind you," most of us still have a rather ambiguous idea of what the mind really is. Poets, psychiatrists and philosophers have each given their own take on the subject (often contradicting one another), and of course, the cliché "Mind, Body and Spirit" finds mention in bookstores and spiritual expos all around the world.

However, for most people, the question is less about what the mind is, and more about what type of influence it has on our daily experience of life. Most of us experience the mind as a continuous and seemingly unstoppable train of thoughts running through our heads. Behind this incessant flow lies a sophisticated web of likes, dislikes, attitudes, habits, inhibitions, morals... and so on and so forth, *ad infinitum*. This often unconscious patchwork determines how we interact and relate to the world around us, giving shape to our joys, grief, pleasures, and fears.

Few indeed have the perception and depth to see the enigmatic strings which bind this mind into a seemingly solid structure. Fewer are those who find ways to articulate it. In "Mind Is Your Business," Sadhguru brings clarity to the conundrum, exploring the possibilities and the pitfalls of the mind, and how it can be cultivated for inner peace, joy, and effectiveness. Compiled from a variety of discourses, this volume weaves together questions posed by seekers over the years – from the probing enquiries of hardened skeptics, to the exasperated pleas of ardent seekers. The questions are diverse, the answers multi-faceted. Addressing the questioner's innate urge to know, Sadhguru answers more than the question posed; he clarifies even the underlying questions that remain unvoiced.

The following pages, laden with Sadhguru's inimitable wit and humor, are a voyage of discovery. Demolishing overused clichés and misconceptions about one's ability to "control the mind" and have "pure thoughts," Sadhguru goes beyond morality and impractical advice, to lay bare the deceptive drama of the mind. He calls the mind a "circus," one that can "render you to the depths of hell within yourself," but that can also "take you to great heights." Meditation, he explains, is not only a powerful device to harness the immense capabilities of the mind, which are left untapped by a majority of human beings, but to access the mystical dimensions of life that are entirely beyond the mind's purview. The whole process of yoga, Sadhguru says, is to give one the ability to use the mind as a tool for one's wellbeing and liberation.

It is this shift – from being a slave to the mind to having the mastery to use it at will – which this book seeks to offer.

English Publications
Isha Foundation

The Circus of the Mind

"Only if you are out of the circus of your mind, you will be hundred percent free of madness."

Why do we refer to the mind as a circus? A circus is not a mess; a circus is a very coordinated activity deliberately made to look like a mess. On one level it is a mess, but on another, it is a highly coordinated activity.

If you look at the way neurons are firing in the brain and what is happening, there is a tremendous sense of cohesiveness in this activity. It is that cohesiveness which is translating into the functioning of the body. A billion things are happening in this body right now simply because there is an extremely well-coordinated play and dance of neurons in the brain. But unfortunately, in most people's experience, the mind has become a mess. It is like a circus, and both aspects of a circus are there. Even the clown in the circus is a highly coordinated gymnast. The outer expression may be that of a clown, but he is extremely talented and balanced in his activity. That is the experience of most people when it comes to their mental activity.

What is the possibility of this circus? This circus can take you to great heights; this circus can also render you to the depths of hell within yourself. Both these possibilities are very alive for every one of us right now. The whole thing is a question of how we conduct this circus and how much of it we take charge of.

Why is it that for one person the mind seems to be a pleasant experience, while for another person the mind seems to be a

Mind Is Your Business

torture device? Why is it that the mind, which is the most miraculous instrument and the most miraculous possibility in our life, has also become such a misery-manufacturing machine? Every kind of misery that human beings are going through is manufactured in their minds. Unable to bear the mental torture, people have invented various kinds of deviations and perversions on this planet just to somehow deal with the mess of the mind. These perversions might give them temporary relief, but after some time the perversions only multiply the mess. They do not really take it away.

Your mind – that which should have been a ladder to the divine – has unfortunately become a stairway to hell, simply because it is too identified with so many things. Once it gets identified, your perception becomes distorted and this distortion permeates every aspect of your life.

People keep telling me, "Sadhguru, for you the biggest thing in your life just happened unasked. Maybe you are chosen. How will it happen to us?" It is not a question of anybody choosing anything for you; it is just that if you keep your intellect unidentified from anything, starting from your body – if you do not even look at yourself as a man or a woman, if you do not identify with your family, your qualifications, your society, your caste, creed, community, nation, or whatever million other identifications that you take on in your life – every human being will naturally lead himself on to his ultimate nature. If we have to experience the circus of the mind as a miraculously coordinated activity rather than as a mess, the most important and crucial thing is that your intellect is not identified with anything. There is no other way.

The intellect is like a scalpel which is constantly cutting through everything. Your ability to discriminate between one thing and the other is purely because of your intellect. You can make a distinction between the floor and the chair only because your intellect is functioning. You know that you must come through the door, not through the wall, only because your intellect is functioning. Without the activity of the intellect, you cannot discriminate.

If a knife has to cut through anything effortlessly and well, it is extremely important that whatever it cuts through does not stick to it. If the residue keeps sticking to the knife, after some time this knife becomes useless. Some of you must have experienced in your kitchens, when you cut an onion with a knife, and then cut mangoes or apples, everything tastes like an onion. Once the residue of what you cut through sticks to the knife, in many ways that knife becomes more of a nuisance than a help. Or in other words, once your intellect identifies with something or the other, it gets chained with the identifications. Once this happens, you have a completely distorted experience of the mind.

Once your intellect gets identified with something, then you get all messed up. This identity is not on one level, it is on many levels. Because of this complex system of identifications, you are in a complex mess.

I must share this with you. I hope it is received with the necessary understanding, because this is about a certain moment of intimacy. I grew up in such a way that right from my childhood, I could remember things that happened when I was just two or three months of age. It just did not allow me to be like a normal child. I thought like an adult. Because of this, nobody could take me on their lap or fondle me or carry me. Even though my brother and sister, who are older to me, were used to being carried and fondled, somehow it was difficult to do those things to me. I always preferred to walk alone and do my own things.

My mother was a very devout and dedicated woman. For her, her whole life was her husband and four children. She never thought about herself. She just gave her life to us. So there was no need for her to ever express, "I love you," or anything. Such a thing was never expected. Whether she loved us or not was never a question that occurred in anybody's mind because her whole life was for us. I developed a kind of relationship with her where though I was the youngest in the family, I was like her elder brother in many ways. She would share things with me that she would not share with anybody else. And when I took advantage of that and joked, she would always say, "Oh, why am I sharing this with you?"

On a certain day when I was just fourteen years of age, because of some interaction, somehow she grew a little tender and expressed her love to me. She was not necessarily saying, "I love you," but somehow she expressed it. For me, For me, it was very matter-of-fact. I just asked her, "If I was born in the next house, would you still feel like this about me?" It hurt her very much. She broke down and went away. I did not intend to hurt her. I just asked a simple question. These questions were constantly going on in me about everything, not just about one thing. And after sometime she came, tears still in her eyes, fell at my feet and went away. I felt that was good for her, some kind of realization happened within her.

I am saying this because our ways of thinking and feeling are so deeply identified with things we are associated with – our body, our parentage, our children, our wife, our husband, our home – with just about anything and everything.

My grandfather used to always eat from a gold-rimmed plate. He was a rich and very proud man. Even when he travelled, another gold plate had to travel with him. Suppose the plate was not there, he just would not eat. The same damn food, what is the problem whether you eat from a gold plate or a steel plate? Okay, so you want to do things in style. But the identification with something as simple as that is so deep that if he ate from another plate, he would become sick. His stomach would be disturbed.

Your identifications are so very deep with big things and small things. Once you are identified like this, your mind is a mess of a circus. It will never rise to any great peak; it will just be a mess. Once you are very deeply identified, it is better not to insult the circus by calling your mind a circus. It is more a "mental diarrhea" because it is just going on nonstop, endlessly. This cannot be stopped with a pill. People have tried drinks, drugs, and all kinds of things, but it cannot be stopped that way. Only when you get dis-identified, when you are able to be involved but not entangled, only then it can stop.

Mind Is Your Business

"Your mind need not be controlled; your mind needs to be liberated."

Mind is not a cap on life, mind is a way to liberate life. Nowadays, everywhere you go, people are saying, "you must control the mind." Your mind does not need to be controlled, your mind needs to be liberated. But unfortunately, people always think of controlling the mind.

People are talking about wanting to be "no-mind." It is a very misunderstood concept. It took millions of years to evolve this mind. Why do you want to become "no-mind" now? It is simply because you are not able to handle the torture of your mind. If your mind was ecstasy, if your mind was the means to your blissfulness, would you want to become a "no-mind?" Only because it has become a mess, and you are seeing it as a barrier, not a stepping stone, you want to become a "no-mind." Mind is not a barrier, it is a tremendous possibility. It is because we are trying to go about handling the mind without addressing and understanding its fundamental nature that this problem has happened.

Morality is the major problem. One of the biggest problems is, right from one's childhood, what is right and what is wrong has been imposed on the mind. People have taught you what is good and what is bad. But good and bad are very, very strong points of identity. You naturally get identified with whatever you consider good, and you are naturally repelled from whatever you consider bad.

Having an aversion to something and an attraction towards something else is the basis of identification. Whatever you are averse to dominates your mind. The nature of your mind is such that if you say, "I do not want something," only that thing keeps happening in your mind. There is no subtraction or division in the mind, there is only addition and multiplication. You cannot take away anything by force from the mind. This does not need any enlightenment to be understood.

If you just close your eyes for a minute and look at it, you can see that you cannot do anything by force in the mind. If somebody tells you, "This is good and that is evil but do not think about the evil," that is a full-time job. Nothing else but that, will be going on in the mind. The moment you label something as good and something else as bad, you getting identified with the good and having aversion to the bad is a natural process.

It is because people realized that identification is causing so much trouble that they immediately started giving you an antidote – "detachment." The moment you detach yourself, your ability to experience life is also gone. Where there is no involvement, there is no life. Life cannot be experienced unless there is involvement – the deeper the involvement, the deeper the experience of life. However small the event may be, however small a piece of life may be, if you are deeply involved, it is a great experience for you. Nothing dramatic or spectacular needs to happen in your life. If you are deeply involved with the simplest aspect of your life, you will see every aspect of your life is spectacular. But why is so much detachment being taught everywhere? It is because of the fear of entanglement. It is from this fear that detachment is always being propagated. If you detach yourself from life, you are avoiding life. You are here to experience life, not to avoid life.

Can you experience life unless you are involved? No. But right now there is a fear of entanglement – "If I involve myself

Mind Is Your Business

maybe I will get entangled." Entanglement has happened because of the discriminatory nature of your involvement – your involvement is coming from a certain identification. "I am involved with this person because this is my wife, this is my husband, this is my child, this is my home..."

It is the identification which is causing entanglement, not the involvement. If your involvement is beyond your identifications, you will see that involvement brings absolute joy to life. If your involvement is indiscriminate, you would simply be involved with all life around you in just the same way – with the very air that you breathe, with the very land that you stand on. Involvement enhances life in a tremendous way. If life is not enhanced within you, all the higher possibilities of life will also never happen to you.

In the process of becoming spiritual or trying to be spiritual, a lot of people have become like goats because if you practice how not to be involved with life, you will slowly become more lifeless. You will become less of life as days go by – too much of mind and very little of life. As life recedes in you, you will see nothing fantastic can ever happen. Only if life is happening exuberantly within, can it carry you to higher possibilities.

"Your aliveness is going down because you are committing suicide in instalments."

Involvement need not necessarily mean that you have to go and do something. You can just look at people and be involved. You can look at the sky and be involved. You can look at every life and be involved. You can close your eyes and still be involved. Involvement is not an act, it is a certain willingness towards life – you have become willing to the process of life. If you get identified, you are becoming unwilling to the process of life – you are only willing in selection, you are not willing with the rest of life. It is this unwillingness which is scaling down the aliveness in a human being.

Just look at yourself and see, when you were five years of age how alive you were and today how alive you are. Your aliveness has gone down, hasn't it? Really gone down! With age our physical capabilities may go down, but aliveness need not go down. Even if you are a hundred years old, you can be as alive as a child.

Your aliveness is going down because you are committing suicide in instalments by becoming selective in your involvement. Whatever you do willingly, that is your heaven. Whatever you do unwillingly, that is your hell. What is considered so beautiful can become so horrible; what is a great love affair, becomes rape if it happens to you when you are unwilling. The difference is just willingness and unwillingness. If you take away the willingness, the process of life naturally becomes a suffering.

Whether your mind is a misery or your mind is a miracle simply depends on whether you are allowing life to happen to you absolutely willingly or unwillingly. Is your life a love affair or is life just raping you? That is the question. If you are being raped by life, then the mind is a misery. If your life has become a love affair, then life is blissfulness, and the mind too is blissfulness.

If the circus of the mind has to become a symphony and rise to its crescendo, you cannot be selectively involved. In the circus, the trapeze bars and trapeze ropes are always tied in such a way that the trapeze artists will get to reach each other only if they go full swing. If any one of them is a little unwilling, the circus will collapse. They must go all out – otherwise it cannot happen in a beautiful way. That is so with you also. Are you going all out with life? If you are going all out, that itself will settle the mind.

The passion with which you look at your lover or your child, with the same passion, look at the sky, the trees, the earth, or anything. If you have the same passion and involvement with every aspect of your life, the mind is not a misery. It is a beautiful circus. "Circus" is not a negative word. A circus is a hugely coordinated symphony of actions. And that is how the brain is functioning. The accumulated mass of information is what we generally refer to as the mind, and its activity comes from that very information. This information has a basis beyond your birth.

From the moment you are born to this moment, everything that you have seen, heard, smelled, tasted, touched, everything that you have perceived through the five sense organs is recorded in your mind. Whether you consciously recorded this, whether it happened in wakefulness or sleep, it is still recorded. This can be very easily checked. Suppose you are fast asleep and somebody says something to you, if we do certain processes, you will see that what you heard in sleep is still there, and you can very easily repeat it. These things have been done as experiments in hypnotized conditions. But in the yogic system, we have always been aware of this.

In India, we always knew that the best time to put the best input into a human being is when he is in the mother's womb. So elaborate care was taken about how a pregnant woman should be, in what kind of atmosphere she should be, and under what kind of influence she should, and should not come. She was not even allowed to meet certain people. Only those people who were most loving, wise, and intelligent were allowed to meet her. She was not exposed to any kind of negative emotions or negative situations because that is the time when you can teach the child which is in deep sleep, and just forming. Because there is such a sense of deep sleep, it is very easy to teach. When a person is awake, there are any number of distractions. While you are being taught, you are aware of the body, you are scratching your body, looking around, and doing this and that. But when you are asleep, all these things are absent. Your absorption is absolute.

So everything that you have heard, seen, smelled, tasted and touched, in wakefulness or in sleep, is recorded. This information is there. How harmoniously we use this information reflects the effectiveness of the mind. Or how much of a mess this information becomes depends on the ineffectiveness or the mess of the mind.

To organize this, people have done various things. All kinds of methods and exercises are being tried out in the world. Yes, there are many ways to make minor corrections and make yourself a little more effective than before, but if you really want to unleash the mind – not control the mind – if you truly want to unleash the power of the mind, the fundamental thing is, your intellect should not be identified with anything. Then your perception comes to such clarity that the mind naturally organizes itself, nobody has to organize the mind. Only because the perception is so distorted, its function and its outcome are also distorted.

"Once you liberate your mind from being identified with anything, then mind is a miracle; mind is a spectacular circus, not a mess."

In South India, there was a king called Krishnadevaraya. He had a jester, Tenali Ramakrishna.

One day, the royal barber was giving Krishnadevaraya a haircut. A crow came and sat there and started making its usual "ka-ka" sounds. The barber stopped the haircut and with arrested attention, started listening to the crow. Krishnadevaraya looked at him and said, "What is this? You are listening to the crow as if you can understand what the crow is saying."

He said, "Wait, Your Majesty, wait. He has a message," and very carefully listened for a long time. Then he shook his head.

Krishnadevaraya became very curious. "What is this? You understand crows?"

"Yes."

"What is he saying?"

"Your Majesty, this crow has come as the messenger of your forefathers from heaven. What he is saying is that they are in heaven, but uncared for. Everything is physically taken care of, but there is nobody to entertain them. They are really longing for some help from you. That is why they have sent this crow as a messenger. We must send somebody to heaven to entertain your forefathers. How can we leave them not entertained like that?"

Krishnadevaraya immediately became very emotional. "My forefathers are bored and suffering because of a lack of attention and entertainment? I must send the best entertainment. Let us see who is the best dancer, the best musician, the best…"

Then a few other courtiers arrived and each of them said, "Oh, Your Majesty, I am willing to go, but I can't sing for nuts. But if you want me to go and serve your forefathers, I will go to heaven and serve right now." Like this they built it up. But then they said, "No, for your forefathers we must send the best of the best. How can we send a musician? How long can he entertain them? If they hear him for two days, they will be finished with him. If you send a dancer, how long will she entertain them? If you see her for a few days, you are done. We must send somebody who can keep them continuously entertained. Who better than Tenali Ramakrishna? He can keep your forefathers entertained forever because he is so ingenious. He is the best person."

Krishnadevaraya also agreed that there was nobody like Tenali Ramakrishna. "He is the best entertainer. I would not like to part with him, but my forefathers…" He was feeling very emotional. He said, "Yes, we will send Tenali Ramakrishna."

Tenali Ramakrishna was called, and he heard the story of how he should go to heaven to serve the forefathers. Immediately, he put on the same act, "Oh, Your Majesty, I am more than willing. This is such an honor. I am going. I know the whole process of how to go."

The barber had also received instructions as how to send the man to heaven – the crow had instructed him. The barber said, "You must make the man sit facing south, and then you must get lots of sandalwood, camphor, and ghee. The heap should rise well above a full-grown elephant. It should be only sandalwood, pure ghee, and camphor. Keep the man inside this whole heap and then set fire to it. This fire should burn for a minimum of three days, and then the man will evaporate and go to heaven and serve the forefathers."

Tenali Ramakrishna said, "This is the correct method. This is the best way. I will go and serve your forefathers. But let me make the preparation. I want to purify my body, my mind and everything before I go there. I want to take off all the *doshas*[1] in me. Give me just thirty days' time."

A grand site was prepared. Tenali Ramakrishna personally went and supervised the whole process and set up the whole thing with his trusted labor. Krishnadevaraya was moved by Tenali Ramakrishna's dedication towards his forefathers, and his willingness to go to heaven.

The appointed day came and Tenali Ramakrishna went into a haystack first. Over the haystack, this whole "hill" of wood, ghee, and camphor was built, and set on fire. It was kept burning for three days. After three days, nothing but ashes were left. Tenali Ramakrishna had disappeared. Many months passed. Krishnadevaraya wondered what was happening to his forefathers because the damn crow did not come again to tell them what was happening. Every day when the crow came, he asked the barber, "What is he saying, what is he saying?"

But the barber said, "This is not that crow. This is just an ordinary crow, not the messenger crow."

After eight months, one day when Krishnadevaraya was in the full assembly of the court, Tenali Rama arrived with long hair and a long beard. He bowed down to Krishnadevaraya. Krishnadevaraya was overjoyed that Tenali Rama had come back from heaven and said, "What is happening? Are my forefathers well? Did you keep them happy?"

---

1   Defect or blemish. Specifically refers to defects in the physical, mental or energy bodies.

Mind Is Your Business

"I kept them very happy. They have been splitting their sides with my jokes. They are really enjoying everything. It is just that they have one problem, Your Majesty."

"What is that?"

Tenali Ramakrishna said, "There are no barbers in heaven. Look at me, even I could not have a shave. And for your forefathers it has been so many years that they are tripping over their own beards. It has become so difficult that they are carrying long beards around their necks and are really having a problem. They need a good barber. We must send them the best barber in the land."

Of course, the best one is the royal one. Krishnadevaraya immediately said, "I will send my personal barber."

The barber quaked. He fell at Krishnadevaraya's feet and admitted everything.

Once you are identified with something, your perception gets so distorted. From the day you were born, to increase your identity with your family, your parents have been campaigning that you belong to them. To increase your loyalty to your community, caste, creed and religion, other people have been campaigning. To increase your loyalty to your country, some other people are campaigning. On different levels, people are constantly campaigning to ensure that you are deeply identified with something, so that you will serve those purposes.

I want you to know, a campaign can be run to make you believe just about anything. If we campaign hard enough, we can make you worship anything, hate anything, love anything, and give up your life for anything. We just have to work on your identifications. How strong your identity is, and how far you are willing to go. People get so identified because of these campaigns and everything gets distorted.

Nobody wants you to be a liberated human being because they are afraid of freedom. They believe that if someone is free, he may do irresponsible things. If someone is truly free, why would he do anything irresponsible or harmful? Someone does irresponsible things only because he is not free – he is not free in his mind, he is too identified with himself and nothing else. That is why he can harm somebody else. If he is not identified even with himself, no harm can come out of such a human being.

It is this distinction which has unfortunately been misinterpreted as non-attachment or detachment. Detachment does not mean that you detach yourself from your family or the people and life around you. Detaching yourself from your family is very easy. When they become inconvenient, you can detach yourself. That is not detachment. Detachment means you have disentangled yourself from the process that you call "body," and from the process that you call "mind," because both these things are accumulations from outside.

The body is something that you gathered. It is an accumulation of the food that you have eaten – breakfast-lunch-dinner, breakfast-lunch-dinner, breakfast-lunch-dinner… and snacks. Similarly, what you call as "my mind" is also an accumulation. All the impressions that you received through the five sense organs became the mind. Whatever you accumulate can be yours, but it can never be you. If there are these two sets of accumulations, naturally there must be something more fundamental than these within you.

The whole system and technology of yoga is not a teaching, a philosophy, a belief system, or a religion. It is a whole technology to go beyond the limitations of your accumulations and experience that dimension which is fundamental to these accumulations. What we offer as Inner Engineering[2] is fundamentally just this. If you go into these processes, there will be a distinct separation between what is you, your body, and your mind. Once this little space between you and the activity of the mind and body arises, the mind is no longer a mess. It is a great symphony. It is a tremendous possibility that can take you to great heights.

---

2   The basic program offered by Isha Foundation, providing tools for an individual to re-engineer himself from within, including transmission of the powerful Shambhavi Mahamudra.

The Garbage Bin

"Mind is not in any one place. Every cell in this body has its own intelligence. The brain is sitting in your head, but mind is all over the place."

Questioner: Are "mind" and "brain" the same thing?

Sadhguru: No, they are not. Like your little finger, the brain is also another part of your body – with a different function, of course. Can the mind be active without a brain? It is not just the brain. The mind cannot be active without many things. We need not scoop out your brains to take away the activity of your mind. That can be done in so many ways.

The brain is a physical thing. It is the body. It has a certain function which is essential for the mind to exist. But the mind is a certain consequence and activity. For example, suppose you are speaking. Your speech exists. If you stop speaking and sit quietly, where is your speech? Is it sitting and waiting in your mouth? No. It just does not exist. Your speech exists only when you are in that activity. Otherwise, it does not.

Similarly with your mind, your mind exists only in its activity. If you take off the activity, it does not exist. It is not a physical object. Where is your mind? If you knew where it was, you would have fixed it by now. You don't know where it is because it exists only in its activity. But brain is a physical object. The brain is not only about thoughts and the other things which you refer to as "mind." It also controls how your liver, your heart, even how your little finger should function.

Mind Is Your Business

They are two different things, but are they connected? Definitely – everything is connected. Every cell in your body is connected. Every cell in your body has its own mind. Your genes carry memory and act out that memory. That is a kind of a mind.

In yoga, we look at a human being as five sheaths of body. Three are physical realities; the other two are in a different realm. The three – physical body, mental body and energy body – are all physical, and they cannot exist without each other. The physical body is physical, you can see it. But there is a mental body that you cannot see. Every cell in this body has its own intelligence; this is a mental body. The brain is sitting in your head, but the mind is not in any one place, it is all over the place. It is a certain activity. If you cease the activity, then the mind does not exist.

If you turn off the mind, it is not just off – it ceases to exist. If you turn it on, it is again there. It is like a cinema. When a cinema is on, it is more real than real. Then, with just one switch, it vanishes. It does not matter whether a war scene is going on or a love scene is going on, you turn off one power switch, it is gone. Mind is just like that. A big drama is going on which is so real. In your experience of life, what is going on in your mind is more important to you than what is going on outside of you. What your thought and emotion says, is far more important than what the world is saying. But if you turn it off, it suddenly ceases to exist. Then you see the ridiculous nature of your mind. It creates such a drama, but it is actually so fragile. It is like a cinema – you turn it off, it is finished.

If it becomes a conscious cinema, there is no problem. There is nothing wrong with the cinema. Let us say you have a DVD in your house and all the walls in your house are screens. If the same movie is playing all the time, won't it drive you to distraction? It will drive you to madness, and that is what going on right now.

When the mind is out of control, we say that person is mad. I am not saying your movie is bad. It does not matter what kind of movie it is, if it is on all the time, it is a horror. You can enjoy the movie only if you can turn it on and turn it off when you want. Then it is a wonderful movie.

"If you try to make the limited unlimited, you will suffer."

Questioner: I don't know if I am strange but I think most people are like this. We spend a lot of our energy and life thinking about sexuality and the other sex. I would like to hear something from you about this.

Sadhguru: There is nothing strange about it. It is just that your intelligence has been hijacked by your hormones. It is not you, it is just a compulsive behavior.

When you were a child, it didn't matter to you what reproductive organs a man or a woman carried. But the moment hormones started playing within you, you could not think of a world beyond that. And you will see, beyond a certain age, when the play of hormones goes down, once again it doesn't matter. When you look back, you cannot believe you were the one who was doing all that.

Right now you are thinking about the opposite sex all the time. Let us say I grant you the boon that all the women in the world will be after you. You will still live an unfulfilled life. It will definitely not get you anywhere worthwhile. I am not trying to make it dirty. It is fine, but you will live within the ambit of the physical body. Maybe a little bit of pleasure will come to you but it is not the ultimate. No matter what you have or how much you have, you will still live an unfulfilled life. You may try to manage it somehow with a little bit of emotion, a little bit of mind, and a little bit of society, but it does not matter what you do, if you are sincere with your life, you will see you are still living an unfulfilled life.

If you live within the ambit of the body, it knows only survival and procreation, nothing else. There is nothing wrong with that, it is just limited, that is all. The truth is, the physical body has to play only that much of a role in your life. But now you are trying to stretch it all over. You will definitely bring suffering to yourself because you are trying to create falsehood. People who think they are just perfect and that nothing will ever happen to them, look at what happens to them after some time. Life has its ways – a million different ways, the most unexpected ways – to bend you, break you, knead you, and grind you. Have you seen it happening to people around you? If life situations do not break you, death will.

Every moment of your life, every step, no matter how many places you think you are going, whether you are going to your office, your home or on a vacation, the body doesn't know all that – it is walking straight to the grave. Every moment, it is going nowhere else. Right now because you are young, because of the play of hormones, you have forgotten this. But slowly, as time passes, it will become more and more apparent that the body is walking towards the grave.

If all that you have known is just the body and you are going to lose the whole of it, fear becomes the way to live. The physical body's ways are very limited. If you try to make it everything, if you try to make the limited unlimited, you will suffer because that is the way of the body. There is no other way.

There is nothing wrong with your hormones, it is just that they are compulsive. Once you live a compulsive life, you are living the life of a slave. Do you want to be a slave? There is something within you which cannot be a slave. Whether you

Mind Is Your Business

are a slave to something or somebody, once you are a slave, unknowingly, slowly, you will become a long face. When you were a child, you were full of big smiles because there wasn't so much slavery. Slowly, as different kinds of compulsions took over, without knowing why, although everything – your business, your family, your relationships – is going fine in your life, your face is becoming longer and longer. You are doing desperate acts to be happy. As people get richer and older, you will see, they start doing more desperate things to be happy.

Desperation comes because you are trying to make a small aspect of your life into everything. It will not work. Today, western cultures, especially, have made the body into everything – and their suffering is untold. Physically, everything is well and properly arranged – food, healthcare, insurance, cars. But people are suffering immensely. Almost every fifth person is on some kind of medication just to maintain mental balance. If you have to take a tablet every day to remain sane, that is not joyfulness, isn't it? You are on the verge of breaking down every day because you have made a small aspect of your life the whole of life. Life is just taking its toll, nothing else. So don't go that way. Everything has to play only as much of a role as it has to play in your life. If you try to make it the whole, it will not work.

"If you simply sit here as a piece of life – not as a man or a woman, not as a Hindu or a Christian, not as an Indian or an American, not as anything – simply as a piece of life, you will see, the mind will become still."

Questioner: How do we keep our thoughts pure?

Sadhguru: Who told you that a thought can be dirty? A thought is just a thought. It is neither pure nor dirty. It is simply because you get identified with it that it looks like reality. Every thought that you have is happening only from the information that you have already gathered, the influences that you have come under, and the data that you have collected within yourself. No new thought is happening to you. You can mix it and make permutations and combinations out of it, but nothing new ever comes out of you because what you name as "my mind" is not really your mind. Your mind is just society's garbage bin. Everybody who comes your way, throws some nonsense into your head and goes. You do not have a choice about what to receive and what not to receive. Can you say, "I don't like this person. I don't want anything from him." Is it possible? If you don't like him, he will throw more into your mind and go. So what you call as "my mind" is just an accumulation.

When I say garbage bin, I am not saying it is useless. For example, your home can probably do without a television, maybe even without a telephone, but it definitely cannot do without a garbage bin. The quality of your house is very much decided

Mind Is Your Business

by the garbage bin. But because it is such a useful device in your house, suppose you decided to sleep in it tonight, then it becomes terrible.

This is all that has happened to you right now. You are sleeping and living inside the garbage bin, so it seems difficult. If you keep the garbage bin elsewhere, open it and use it when you have to, or shut it when you don't want it, this would be a wonderful instrument. The problem is that you are stuck in it all the time.

There is nothing wrong with the content of your mind. You better have all the filth in the world in your mind, otherwise if you don't know what is what, you may walk into it, by accident or by somebody's intention. But if you know, you will know this is not for me. So, there is nothing wrong with the content of your mind if you do not get identified with it. If you get identified with it, it makes you feel filthy because everything in the world is there in your mind and now it is sticking to you. If you just keep it where it should be, there is really no problem.

If you want to ignore the content of your mind, if you are willing, one thing you can do is, just say, "I am stupid." If you are stupid, you will not attach any significance to your thought. If you think, "I am very smart," you will attach too much importance to your thought. You just have to see, "I am quite stupid."

It takes a lot of intelligence to see "I am stupid." The difference between a stupid person and an intelligent one is that an intelligent person knows he is stupid, but an idiot does not. Look at it in terms of existence and you. If you look at with what organization, capability and certainty a simple ant is conducting its life, you will see that you are quite stupid. Have you seen, even a simple ant – such a tiny thing – is dead sure of what he wants with his life. He knows what to eat, what not to eat, what is nourishing for him, what is not. He does not read that micro-print on the back of the package. He just knows what he wants.

If you look at every life, if you look at how every atom is functioning, you will realize you are stupid. Everything in existence is happening with a phenomenal sense of intelligence. The very soil you walk upon is tremendously intelligent. If you plant a mango seed and a neem seed, the mango produces sweetness, the neem produces bitterness. It is the same soil. Has the land ever become a little confused and made mangos come out of a neem seed? Everything is spot on. Even inanimate things are dead sure of what they are doing. The only confused fool is a human being.

If you know "I am stupid," then you will not attach too much importance to your thought and you will start looking at life. If you start looking at life more, your intelligence will definitely flower. Then, thought is not a process, thought is not a problem, because not much thought will be there. If you don't pay any attention to your thought, it will just die. Don't pay attention to it. But you cannot stop paying attention to it unless you think or see that your thoughts are so petty and quite stupid compared to the rest of the existence. Without a single thought on their mind, an ant, a bird, and a bee all just know what to do.

If you become like this, once in a way when you consciously think, it will be crystal clear. It will be like a knife which cuts through everything. Right now, thought is all over the place, so it has no penetration. If you rest it, once in a way when you pull out your sword, it will cut through everything. But if you are doing this with everything that comes your way all the time, your sword will become like a stick. You must keep it sheathed. Then, when you pull it out when you need it, it is a useful weapon.

So don't try to have pure thoughts. Pure thoughts are most dangerous because you will get terribly attached to them. What is a pure thought? Is there such a thing? There is nothing pure or impure about a thought. Whatever the content of your mind, it just throws itself out. Don't pay any attention to it unless you consciously bring it forth. If you consciously generate a thought, that is different. Then you will naturally create the kind of thought you want. Otherwise, these thoughts are just random happenings. That should stop.

If thoughts are going on continuously, if you are having mental diarrhea, you obviously ate some bad food. You have physical diarrhea because you eat bad food. If you have mental diarrhea, you obviously consumed something wrong. The moment you identify yourself with something that you are not, you are finished – your mind is in a continuous run. There is no other way. Do what you want, try as hard as you want, it is not going to stop. But if you take away these identities, if you simply sit here as a piece of life – not as a man or a woman, not as a Hindu or a Christian, not as an Indian or an American, not as anything – simply as a piece of life, you will see, the mind will become still. Now, when you want to think, you can think, but if you don't want to think, you don't think. That is how it should be.

If I want to move my hand, I move my hand. If I don't want to, I keep it still. This is a useful body. Suppose it was moving all the time, wouldn't this be a crazy body? If the same thing is happening to your mind, is that not a crazy mind? Your only comfort is that others cannot see it. If your body did it, everybody could see it. When your mind does it, everybody cannot see it, but people can see it if they watch you close enough. If someone is a little aware, they can very clearly see it.

"The main aspect of meditation is, as you become more meditative, you become the boss, your mind becomes the slave, and that is how it should always be."

Questioner: Whenever I try to meditate, my mind always seems to come up with excuses not to meditate and I end up getting distracted. I just don't seem to be able to sit still and meditate. How do I deal with this?

Sadhguru: Your mind does not like meditation. When you want to sit and meditate, the mind will do everything to see that you don't. First it will say, "Oh, we'll meditate tomorrow." "Tomorrow" is the deepest cunning of your mind. The mind will not say, "I won't do it." If your mind says, "I won't do it," your ego will say, "I will do it." That is the nature of your ego. If I want to get something done by you, one simple way of getting it done is to say "Please don't do it. No, you should not do it. Don't do it." You will do it because that is the nature of the ego. So the mind will never say, "I will not do it." It will say, "Let's do it tomorrow" – and tomorrow never comes.

In the rural areas of South India, there is a belief that evil spirits try to enter your house in the evenings, and because these evil spirits can only see the color red, they go for your blood. So people write *"naale baa"* in red paint on the front door. *"Naale baa"* means, "come tomorrow." Every day, the evil spirit supposedly comes to the doorstep, sees this sign and thinks, "Oh, this house is for tomorrow," and goes away. Tomorrow never comes, so the evil spirit never enters the house. People have done this to so many things that they should be doing in their life. They have done, "*naale baa, naale baa*" to their very happiness.

When you sit for meditation, if the mind's "come tomorrow" tactic fails, if you say, "No, no, I am committed. I must sit for meditation. I'll just settle down," the mind will try its next trick. Suddenly, that telephone number that you have been trying to remember for the last one week will flash bright and clear in your mind. If you say "Eureka!" jump up, and run to the telephone, the meditation is finished.

If you don't run off, but continue to sit and meditate, in two to three minutes, in half a dozen different places, you will suddenly start to itch. If you don't meditate, nothing will happen, but if you sit for meditation, so many things will start happening everywhere. This is because the mind knows that if you keep the body still, the mind will also naturally become still. And the mind knows that if it allows this to happen, it will become enslaved. This is why in yoga, so much stress has been laid on *asanas,* because if you just learn how to keep your body absolutely still, then your mind will also become still.

If you just observe yourself, you will see how many unnecessary movements your body is making when you stand, sit, and speak. If you look at your life and see, you will see that probably more than half the time is taken up in this. There is so much unnecessary thought and activity with the body – things that you yourself do not really care for. But if you keep the body still, slowly the mind will start collapsing.

This is when your mind will play the final trick. It asks the question, "What will I get? What is the takeaway from this meditation?" That is the key to all the activity that is happening in the mind. It is all about "What can I get?" If you drop this calculation, ninety percent of the work is over, spiritually. Another ten percent will happen by itself. You don't have to get anything. You don't have to benefit from it. This is not about becoming healthy or becoming enlightened or reaching heaven – this is just wasting time. Just learn to waste some time meditating every day. Nothing needs to happen. If you look for the takeaway, you will only take petty things. The real thing will never come with you. If you want the real thing, you just have to drop this one simple calculation. If you just pull the plug, if you just destroy this one calculation, the very foundations of the mind are taken away. Suddenly it is different, it becomes a wonderful slave.

Right now your mind is the boss, you are the slave. The main aspect of meditation is, as you become more meditative, you become the boss, your mind becomes the slave, and that is how it should always be. The mind is a terrible master. He will put you through all kinds of endless suffering. But the mind is a wonderful slave. If you keep your mind in a certain way, you can do anything you want with it.

A Ladder to the Divine

"If you want to know life in its immensity, you need something more than your thoughts, your logic, or your intellect."

Questioner: What does it mean to be aware?

Sadhguru: "Awareness" is a very vague term. It means different things to different people. When we say "awareness," do not mistake this for mental alertness. Mental alertness will help you to survive better. It will help you conduct your survival process in a slightly superior fashion. Awareness is not something that you do. Awareness is aliveness. Your aliveness is only because of your awareness. If you were completely unaware, would you know that you are alive? You are alive only to the extent you are aware. And to what extent you are aware, only to that extent something is in your experience.

"How do I practice awareness?" You cannot practice it. How can you practice life? If you were dead you could practice life. If you are alive, how can you practice life? It is just that right now, you are not giving much room for your aliveness to happen because you have given too much significance to what you think and feel. Your psychological process has become far more important than your life process. Why awareness seems to be so difficult is simply because we have let our minds go into endless chatter. If your mind is not chattering, awareness is the natural way to be.

People have made their thought process so important. They have even gone to the extent of saying, "I think, therefore I am." Which do you think is true: you think because you exist, or you exist because you think? You can generate a thought because you exist, isn't it? We want to shift the significance to the life process. You can play with your psychological process whichever way you want, but it is only because you are alive that you can think.

Once in a while, if I just close my doors and sit in a place for five days, I do not have a single thought for five days. I don't look out of the window, I don't read, I don't do anything. I am simply being alive. This is such a huge phenomenon happening within you, what is there to think about? Being alive is a far bigger process than your stupid thought process.

Anyway, what can you think? You are just recycling the nonsense that you have gathered. Can you think something other than the nonsense that has been fed into your head? You are just recycling the old data you have gathered. This recycling nonsense has become so important that you can even dare to say "I think, therefore I am," and that becomes the world's way of life. Existence *is*, even without your silly thoughts.

If you choose, you can fully be and still not think. Please see, the most beautiful moments in your life are those moments when you were not thinking about anything. What you call moments of bliss, moments of joy, moments of ecstasy, moments of utter peace, these were moments when you were not thinking about anything but were just living.

Which is more important, living or thinking? You must decide this – do you want to be a living being or a thinking being? Right now, ninety percent of the time, you are only thinking about life, not living life. Are you here to experience life or to think about life? You want to experience life, and you cannot experience life if you are lost in your thought. It is only through perception that you experience. You cannot experience through thought. With the past experience of life, you are cooking up something in your head – that is a thought process. Whatever you think has no significance because your thoughts have nothing to do with reality. They do not mean anything. Everybody can think up their own nonsense whichever way they want. It need not have anything to do with reality at all.

Your psychological process is a very small happening compared to the life process. Isn't being alive right now more important for you than thinking? But if I trample upon your thought even a little, you are even willing to die for it. People die for their ideas. People die for their thought. People die for what they believe in. Thought has become far more important than the life process because people have not realized the immensity of what it means to be alive. Because life has been restrained within the survival activity, thought looks grander than life. But it is not so. Thought is just a small happening compared to the life process.

Aristotle is considered as the father of modern logic. His logic is very simple and straight – A can only be A, B can only be B. A cannot be B, B cannot be A. Can you argue with this? Logically it looks perfect. But let us look at this.

You are here either as a man or a woman. But how did you come here? Because a man and woman came together. Now suppose you are a woman, does it mean to say your father has made no contribution to you? He does exist within you, doesn't he? Suppose you are a man, does it mean your mother made no contribution to you? Doesn't she exist within you? The fact is that you are either a man or a woman, but the truth is you are both. Truth is that dimension which is not logically explainable. It does not fit into logic because logic is always dividing, truth is always unifying. So where will this logic fit into life?

If you apply your logic too much to your life, all life will be squeezed out of you. The logical aspect of the mind is useful only to handle the material realities of life. If you try to handle yourself with logic, you will be a total mess because fundamentally, if you look at your life absolutely logically, there

Mind Is Your Business

is no meaning to it. When you wake up in the morning tomorrow, think absolutely logically. Don't look at the sunrise, don't look at the birds in the sky, don't think of someone you love, your child's face, or the flowers in the garden. Just think logically. Now, you actually have to get out of bed – that is not a small feat. You go to the toilet, brush your teeth, eat, do some work, eat, work, eat, sleep – tomorrow morning, same thing – over and over again. You have to do this for the next 40, 50 years. Think 100% logically, without looking at your life's experience – is it really worthwhile?

Moments of extreme logic are moments of suicide, please see this. If we think hundred percent logically about life, there is really no reason to live; there is really no reason for you and me to exist here. But if you look at one beautiful moment of your life's experience, suddenly everything is sparked up and you want to live. The logical aspect of your life and the experiential dimension of your life are diametrically opposite to each other. That is why you are struggling with it. If you look at life experientially, there is every reason to live. If you look at life logically, there is no reason to live.

Why does someone commit suicide? Because they refuse to look at the experiences that they have had. If they fail an examination, people commit suicide; their husbands left them, they commit suicide; they lost their property, they commit suicide. People do it for so many reasons. Let's say, today your husband or your wife left you. If you think logically, "My whole life was to love this person and be with this person, and now this person is gone. Where is the reason for me to live?" If you go logically, you will commit suicide. But if your husband or wife is gone, maybe it is a whole new possibility in your life. Maybe things that you could never imagine will happen to you simply because you are free from one aspect of life. We do not know, but it is possible.

If you think hundred percent logically, there is really no possibility of life. Only if you know to what extent your logic should go and where it should not go, your life will be beautiful. If you become absolutely logical, there is no beauty to your life. Everything becomes bare and no good.

Logic is essential only to handle the material aspect of life. If you want to know the experiential dimensions of life, you will never know it with your petty thought. Even if you have Einstein's brain, it is still a petty thought because thought cannot be bigger than life. Thought can only be logical, functioning between two polarities. That is too small. If you want to know life in its immensity, you need something more than your thoughts, your logic, or your intellect. Only if you open up that dimension, you will taste life in its larger proportion. Otherwise, you will know only the physicality of life. With thought, you can know the physical and use the physical, but you will not penetrate anything other than the physical.

It is because the world has given so much significance to Aristotle and his tribe that all the sciences have developed in the physical dimension. With this, much comfort has come. You may be thrilled about how many things your computer or the internet can do, but if you really look at it, it has not done anything to your life. It has brought comfort and convenience, but ultimately, it has not brought you any joy. It has not taken you to any higher dimension of experience or existence. You are in the same place. Instead of riding a bullock cart, maybe you are driving a Mercedes or dreaming of one. Whichever way, you are still only moving from point A to point B. You have not gone to another point. Whether you fly a jet plane or a bullock cart, it is only lateral movement. Even if you take a spacecraft, it is still only from point A to point B.

In spite of all this exploration, no new dimension has occurred to you because the instruments of exploration that you are using are too limited. They are just logical and intellectual, so there is no way you will touch any other dimension of life. It is not possible. I appreciate the enthusiasm, but it is as if you were trying to go to the moon with a bullock cart. It does not matter how hard you beat the bulls, it is not going to get there. If you beat the bulls really hard, maybe you can climb a mountain on the bullock cart, but you cannot go to the moon. Either you learn this out of your intelligence, or life will maul you and teach you a lesson slowly. The choice is yours.

"One should use information and logic as a drunkard would use a lamp post, only for support, not for illumination."

Questioner: If to perceive the mystical, one has to drop the logical, how does a gnana yogi progress and attain on the path? Isn't that path all about using the logical mind and dissecting things?

Sadhguru: If your logical intellect could grasp it, why would you call it mystical? What we refer to as the mystical has become mystical only because it is not within the grasp of the logical intellect.

A *gnana* yogi is someone who uses his intellect to start with, and then moves on to use his intelligence. If he is just bombastic intellect, he is not a *gnana* yogi. If he is truly a *gnana* yogi, he understands that the logical intellect can never function without information. If you take away all the information from your memory, how will your logic function? Logical intellect is purely an information technology, and information is something that you gather from outside. The only means of gathering information is the five sense organs, and sense perception is not reliable. They have told you, "Seeing is believing." Seeing is not believing – everybody sees what they want to see.

Sense organs can perceive everything only in comparison. If you had not seen darkness in your life, you would not know what light is. It is only in comparison that you know what light is. Now you see a little boy walking around. He is small for you, but that is not the truth. The ant which is crawling on the ground experiences him as a giant. Your ideas of small and big, your ideas of light and darkness, your ideas of good and bad, are all depending upon what you are identified with. Because you are identified with this human body, a dinosaur is big and an ant is small. But that is not the reality. Whatever you experience is only in comparison, which is good for survival, but it does not give you a perception of reality the way it is.

Modern neurosciences say that whatever you may be looking at, you are never seeing it the way it is. Your eyes are not like cameras. Your eye just grasps information and categorizes this information into twelve different aspects. These twelve different aspects go into twelve different parts of your brain where they all get assimilated, and your brain creates an image. What they are saying is, the way you think the world looks is not the way it is. This is not philosophy or mysticism; this is neurology. They are also saying that if there is no past information in your mind, you actually cannot see something.

When the first European ship went to North America, the tribal people there could see the people floating on the ocean and coming towards them, but they could not see the ship because they had never seen a ship before. They had no such information within them so they could not see it. They say for more than a month, they could not see the ship. They could see only the people, because without any kind of information within you, your vision cannot happen.

Your logic functions on information. The very nature of information is such that it does not matter what volume of information you gather, information is always limited. There is no such thing as limitless information. Even as modern sciences process information about the existence, we are not getting any closer to knowing anything. We are more bewildered than ever before. Before modern sciences came, in their own simplistic way, people were dead sure of what is what. Now nobody knows anything. So much information has been gathered, but it has not moved you closer to knowing. It has moved you away from knowing because that is the nature of the existence. Fifty years ago, a doctor was just a doctor. Twenty-five years ago, a doctor was not just a doctor; there was one doctor for this and one doctor for that. There were three different doctors that your body needed. Today there are over 100 specialties, so if you really want health, you need to see 100 doctors or more.

Recently, I was with a group of people in Atlanta, and just four days before that I had injured my knee. Someone who was present in the group said, "I want to examine your knee."

I said, "Why?"

He said, "I am a knee doctor."

I said, "Oh, you are an orthopaedist? You study bones?"

He said, "No, I am a knee doctor."

Then I said, "Oh, I didn't know… which knee?" Because it is not far away before you have one doctor for the right knee and one for the left!

As we study and gather more information about life, one day it will happen that for every cell in your body, you need a different doctor, because every cell in the body is so complex that one man cannot grasp the whole of what even one cell is. You will need a combination of doctors for every cell in your body. As science looks deeper into life, as they gather more information, you will become more bewildered about life.

One should use information and logic as a drunkard would use a lamp post – only for support, not for illumination. If you think information is illuminating the life of a *gnana* yogi, you are wrong, because anyway he cannot see anything for nuts. Light blurs him out, light blurs you out. If you are not ready for the volume of light that is coming your way, it always blurs you out.

Mind Is Your Business

A *gnana* yogi is not just an intellectual fool. He is not the "PhD" kind. It is not that I have anything against education. It is just that, all the PhDs utter the word "Guru" like it is a derogatory word. "Oh, your Guru? We don't have anything to do with a Guru."

"Do you know what it is?"

"It doesn't matter – Guru, no."

Everywhere in the world, the more educated people get, the more derogatory the word "Guru" gets. So, I am not saying this is in revenge. It is just that a PhD is celebrating the volume of information he has gathered. A *gnana* yogi is not like that. He understands that his logic and intellect are a support, but not illumination. He knows that clearly.

Logic is like a scalpel. Your intellect is like a scalpel. You can use a sharp intellect to cut things open and look inward. By cutting alone, you will not know – it is only by looking that you will know. Your intellect and logic can only cut, it cannot look. Your logical intellect can do a phenomenal amount of logical circus.

If you are not exposed to the great logical traces on this planet, you are fortunate, but I want you to know that nowhere else in the world have people used their logic with such devastating impact as Indian culture has. This land has seen logic at its ultimate. If you go into the Vedantic philosophy, logic will rise to such a state that it will just freak you out completely. Really using it like a rocket, it takes it to you a place where it makes you dizzy and intoxicated. Then you realize it is not getting anywhere, it is just causing dizziness in your head due to excessive use of logic. Then you understand that this can be used only to slice things open. It is not an instrument of seeing.

To see, you need intelligence, and intelligence is not logical. For example, right now, there are many ways to look at your body. One way to look at this body is, it is a complex chemical factory. There is a certain intelligence, which is managing and conducting this whole dance of chemistry. Are you stupid enough to believe that you could someday logically conduct this whole chemical dance? You cannot manage a single cell in your body that way.

You need to understand the limitation in which the intellect functions, and the distinction in how the intelligence of life functions. What you call as intelligence and what you refer to as Creator are not different. Creator is just pure intelligence. Intelligence beyond logic is Creator, or what you are referring to as God. If you operate just within the limitations and framework of your intellect, you will never know that which we refer to as the Creator. You will just do the circus of life. Life is a circus when your intellect and your body alone are involved. Life is a dance, when the intelligence begins to play its role.

"A devotee has no agenda of his own. His only objective is to dissolve into his object of devotion."

Questioner: Can you talk about the path of bhakti or devotion?

Sadhguru: Devotion is the quickest way to get to the Ultimate, but the way people have become today, with the intellect being brought forth to this level, you cannot be a devotee. A devotee has no agenda of his own. His only objective is to dissolve into his object of devotion. Let us say he is a devotee of Shiva. It means he just wants to merge or die into Shiva. That is all he knows. He is not thinking of living well or becoming rich or going to heaven. Are you like that? No. For you, devotion is a currency for an easier life. Look at the prayers in the world. Ninety-nine percent of them are just saying, "Give me this, give me that; save me, protect me." Isn't it so?

This is not devotion; this is a deal. You are trying to make a stupid deal. If you really want to become a devotee, and attain to the Ultimate through devotion, then you have no agenda for yourself. You do not want life to go your way. You just want to merge with the Ultimate, that is all. If you are like that, devotion is the quickest way to realization. It is very quick.

But today, with all your education and this questioning mind, devotion is out of the question. Please look at it. Are you capable of becoming truly devout towards somebody? No. So don't talk about it. I am not saying there is no element of devotion at all in you. There is. It can serve some purposes, but it cannot be your way to the Ultimate. You can only take small rides on it – you can sit in the temple for ten minutes and say, "Shiva, save me," and you get confidence to go through the next twenty-four hours. To that extent it works. But it cannot be your ultimate journey because your intellect is not willing to bend down to anybody totally, unless you come to a certain level of experience where you naturally progress into becoming a devotee.

At the ashram,[3] it happens that people come as investigators. Slowly, they become students, then they become disciples, then they become devotees. That is a natural progression of life. As their experience becomes deeper and deeper, they have no option. They are too overwhelmed with what is happening. Then they cannot help bowing down completely. Just bowing down and touching somebody's feet is not devotion. You are bending down because there is going to be a benefit. Somebody has told you, if you get blessings from some Guru, things will happen well. Your business will work well or your children will be healthy. So you bend down. It is okay, you get that also. To that extent devotion works for you, but not as an ultimate vehicle to take you beyond.

You have to use other things that you have. You are right now enjoying the circus of the intellect. You like it. Suppose you discover something today, you get very thrilled. You spend your whole lifetime just under that thrill. What you think up is nothing new, because it was always there in nature. If you just had eyes to see, every damn thing that you discover has already been there. Whatever great discovery you have made, the very earth that you walk upon knows it. In America they call it dirt; dirt knows better than your brains. Everything that you know, everything that you re-invent, the planet already knows.

---

3   Sacred dwelling of spiritual seekers under the guidance of a Guru, spiritual Master. Here, referring to the Isha Yoga Center at the foothills of the Velliangiri Mountains, near Coimbatore, Tamil Nadu.

There is no big deal about that, but you are thrilled with the intellect. If you are thrilled with that, let us use the intellect. If you were more of emotion than intellect, or if you were more of body than intellect, or if you were more of energy than intellect, we would have structured things in a different way. Now you are more of intellect and less of other things, and that is why so much talking is happening. You like words, you like the circus of the intellect, so I am putting you through the circus. Just a little better circus than the one you have known till now.

It would be better for you to use the other faculties also now, because devotion is unavailable to you. Not because devotion is bad. Devotion is the quickest way. It has always been, and it always will be. But it means you have to remove yourself – you have to uproot yourself. Only then it works; otherwise it does not work. Today, because the intellect has developed and a certain prominence has come to the intellect, you cannot brush it aside.

Can you just brush your intellect aside and surrender to me? You cannot do it. If you say that you can, it is big bullshit. I know that. I have seen too much life to believe such things. Every other day people are coming to me, "Sadhguru, I am offering my life to you." Millions of people have said this, but it is only a few who really manage that. They are different. All the others, at that moment when their emotions are on the upsurge, they really feel like it. They are not lying. They just don't know the limitations of what they are. I know them very well.

Devotion as an ultimate vehicle will not work in your present state of mind. It is not possible for you. You are too committed to your body and your intellect. You cannot drop them all of a sudden and become a devotee. Devotion as an act is vulgar. Devotion as a way of life is wonderful. If you go the way of devotion, you have to see whether it is something that works for you. It does not work because you are a thinking person. Thinking people cannot be devout.

Instead of that, it is better you develop a little reverence for life around you. When you have this mind, don't talk devotion. If you come to such a point that the experience of life, or somebody's presence has overwhelmed you so much that your mind has just sunk into the background, that what you think and what you feel is no more important, that somebody else has become much more important for you – then devotion is a possibility.

"Your mind is not a solid state, your mind is a fluid. You can make it take on any shape."

Questioner: Why do human beings suffer more than animals?

Sadhguru: Your concern is only about human suffering and human wellbeing, so you notice only that. You do not notice the suffering that animals are going through. People think it is only they who are suffering, but the way human beings are living, they are making everything in the existence suffer. Every day as you walk around, you probably step on a hundred ants. Some of them die, some of them struggle – they are suffering, but you do not know their suffering. Your suffering is only that your legs are aching from having to walk around. It is always a relative perception.

Your suffering, your enjoyment, and your wellbeing are always from your perspective because your experience of life is through you. The seat of your experience is within you, so you see everything only from your context. In that context you are saying humans suffer more than animals. If you were to go and talk to the ants, they would have so many complaints about you and everything else in the world. The ants are suffering much more than human beings are because they are more in number.

But the thing is, animals only suffer physically, if things go wrong. Human beings suffer much more than other creatures because we have a discretionary intellect. Most of a human being's suffering is mental, and mental suffering is self-created.

A human being is an expert at creating suffering for himself and for others. This is because he has a discretionary mind – he can choose to be any way he wants right now. He can make himself joyful or make himself miserable. You can make anything out of your mind. This choice is there at every moment.

Your mind is not a solid state; it is a fluid. You can make it take on any shape. You could look at a tree and say, "Oh! God is living there. How wonderful!" Or you could look at the tree in terror and say, "Maybe devils are hanging around there." There is no end to the mind. You are capable of becoming anything at any given moment. Unfortunately, most people have learned how to make misery out of themselves. That is the problem.

An animal does not have all these problems. If you had come here as any other creature, life would be very simple for you. When a tiger is born, he does not sit and worry, "How should I become a good tiger? Which God should I worship? What university should I go to?" He has none of these problems. If he just finds enough food, he will become a good tiger. He has no fears and insecurities, "Will I really become a good tiger? What if I end up as a housecat?" These kinds of struggles are not there in him. But you were born as a human being. To become a good human being, look at how many things you have to do. And even after doing all these things, you still do not know where you belong. Only in comparison with somebody else can you say, "I am a better man," but by yourself, you do not know where you stand.

This has happened because when you were in animal form, your life was fixed. There was no confusion. Do you see, there is no confusion on the face of an animal? He is clear; he always knows what to do. But with a human being, the more intelligent he becomes, the more confused he gets – every step is a confusion. Only an idiot is dead sure. An intelligent person is constantly confused with every little step that he takes. You may get thoroughly confused just choosing your breakfast because

Mind Is Your Business

once you become human, you are a possibility. Your life is not fixed. This is the freedom that nature has given you – to choose what you want to become. It is not fixing your life the way it has fixed the lives of other creatures. If your life was also fixed like a dog or a bird's life, you would also have lived just eating, sleeping, reproducing, and dying one day. But now, a certain freedom has been given. You can become anything you want. This moment you can become god-like, this moment you can become a brute. Both are possible within you right now.

It is this freedom which is causing all the pain and struggle for a human being. Human beings are not suffering their bondage, they are suffering their freedom, and that is the biggest tragedy. If bondage was the source of misery, it is bad enough, but we could do something about it. All you have to do is break that one bondage that is holding you down. But if freedom becomes the source of misery, what kind of solution can we find?

That which could be a way to being unlimited has become a way to suffering simply because you are unconscious. Freedom is only a problem when you are unaware. If you were aware, the same freedom would be your benediction. Why meditation has been given so much importance is because it is about making you as conscious as possible, so that you don't suffer your freedom – you make use of your freedom to flower into a larger dimension of who you are. Every human being is born with the same possibility, but all of them do not make themselves into the same things even if they are given the same opportunities – because it is conscious, you can make yourself what you want. This moment you can make your life into heaven, or you can make your life into hell. The choice is yours.

There is a very beautiful story. There was a yogi who was old and nearing the end of his life. He went about telling everybody that he was going to heaven. All the other yogis looked at him and wondered, "How does he know he is going to heaven?" But the yogi very confidently went about telling this to everybody in town.

One day, all of them gathered and asked the yogi, "How do you know you will go to heaven? You do not know what's on God's mind, whether he wants to send you to heaven or hell."

The yogi said, "I don't care what's on God's mind. I know what's on my mind. I am going to heaven and that's all."

And that is all it is.

"If you are genuinely hallucinating, it means you are making up things so powerfully in your mind that it seems real. If you create it in your mind and empower it with your consciousness, it can become a live process."

Questioner: How does one know whether they are hallucinating or experiencing reality, especially when they are on the spiritual path?

Sadhguru: Reality can be much more unreal than hallucination. What neuroscientists and physicists are talking today is far more fairytale-ish than anything that you have known as fairy tales. It is so freakish and outlandish. Whenever yogis spoke about this, people thought it was something great. It is just perception; they just described what they saw.

Hallucination means you are making it up so powerfully that you believe it – that is dangerous. If you are genuinely hallucinating, it means you are making up things so powerfully in your mind that it seems real. If you create it in your mind and empower it with your consciousness, it can become a live process.

The whole science of *tantra yoga* is just this. I know if I utter the word "tantra," people are thinking about acrobatic sexuality. It is truly a sacrilege that people who generally visit India for a month or two at the most, become "experts" in *tantra* and write books about it.

Tantra literally means "a technology." Technology is meant for creating what you want. The physical technologies that we know around us are all about creating physical situations the way we want it. When human minds try to create what they want, they will ask for many things. Most of the time, you would be fortunate if your prayers are not answered because if all your prayers were answered, your life would be truly a disaster.

Tantra does not believe in creating what you want in terms of the physical existence around you, but is focused on creating forms and identities which will function way beyond your own intelligence. *Tantra* is essentially focused on creating a mind higher than oneself, making an intelligence beyond one's present capabilities become available. The technology of making this happen was what was known as *tantric* methods. That is, learning to use your body, your mind, and your energies just as instruments of life, so that you become available to a much higher possibility, an intelligence which is way beyond human capabilities.

There are certain elaborate *tantric* designs which are made to train the mind to intricately design something step by step. Even in the yoga programs, we start by saying, "Do it mentally." This is the first step towards *tantra*. You sit here and go on doing it mentally, after some time you do not have to do it physically. Everything that you can get by doing it physically, you can get by doing it mentally. Mentally, you can exercise the body. If you really apply yourself, after some time you will see, you can improve your muscle tone just by doing it mentally, because once your imagination can be coupled with your life energies, it becomes a living reality, it is no more just imagination.

This fundamentally involves two basic steps. One is to have the ability to vividly create every detail of what you want in your mind, and of truly being able to create as the Creator did. The most fundamental thing is to be able to keep your personality out of your imagination, which takes a certain amount of training

Mind Is Your Business

and dispassion about yourself. That is, you do not think much of yourself. It takes a certain amount of *sadhana* and preparation for a person to be like this, that he can extensively use his mind without imposing his personality upon it.

There is a very beautiful incident. In a town in South India, there was a sage whose name was Poosalar. The king of the town built a huge Shiva temple. It took many years to build this temple. The next day was the opening ceremony for his temple, which was his lifetime's ambition. That night Shiva appeared in his dream and said, "I will not be able to come to your temple's inauguration because Poosalar has built another temple in the same town. I need to go there. He is also opening it tomorrow."

The king woke up with a fright, because after he has strived to build this temple for so many years, after so much money and effort, Shiva says he has to go to some other temple built by Poosalar in the same town. "Who is this Poosalar and which is this temple that I do not know about?" So they went searching for Poosalar.

After much search, they found Poosalar, a cobbler by profession, in a small hut. Those days, a cobbler's profession was looked down upon. The king went there and asked, "Where is your temple? Shiva says he is going to go to your temple, not mine. Where is it?"

Poosalar said, "I just built it in my mind."

Every brick, every stone, he slowly built in his mind for many years, and that is more of a reality than what you actually build with stone and brick.

Once you build this, there is another step of empowering and infusing it with life energies so that it becomes a live process by itself. The *tantric* traditions in India have a variety of gods and especially goddesses. These goddesses were created by people. They actually created and infused life into them so that they became live forces. Even today, if you have a certain access code, you can call forth these goddesses and they become a living reality. There is a whole science and a tradition which evolved out of this about how to make a god. The *tantric* traditions acquired mastery over these things. If I go into the details of this, it will be very hard to digest.

Generally, they always created very powerful, hideous forms because the power of these goddesses was such that if they were also pleasant and beautiful, invariably you would somehow get attached to them. Very few people created beautiful forms. Most created absolutely horrific goddesses so that they were there for their calling, but at the same time you would not want to be attached to them simply because of their appearance and their demeanor.

Imagination can do miraculous things. If you have enough control over your life energies and can empower your imagination, it will become a reality. There are many yogis who live in their own worlds with their own kind of planets, earth, everything. They live in a cave, but they have used their imagination and their life energies to create a whole new dimension of life. He lives there happily. A universe is contained inside the cave.

You can actually walk through it, this is what modern physicists are telling you. You can create multiple realities in the same place right here. Today, neuroscientists are saying there are many dimensions of realities happening right here, and in your perception, a complex perception of all this is happening, but you are not able to compute it and make it into a sensible picture.

In yoga, we have always talked about 21 different realities that can happen simultaneously. Right here, right now, there are 21 realities going on without any geographical distance. It is just that it is not in your experience.

For example, suppose I give you a hard knock on your head, you can still see me, but I will get all distorted in your eyes. Your mind is not able to compute the picture. The picture has gotten distorted because the computing process got affected. Even now this is what is happening. You have the information of all the dimensions, but you are unable to compute it. Perception is there, everything that is here is also getting into you, but you are unable to compute it. All you have to learn is a little more computing skills. It takes a little more training.

If one has the necessary stability to remove his persona from the activity that he does, if you can completely eliminate your persona from whatever you do, suddenly you can raise the pitch of your activity to a completely different dimension. But people do not generally know how to act towards something that does not concern them or that they are not involved in – and that is the limitation. That is the terrible crippling limitation that a human being has imposed upon himself. Whatever is not him or his, he cannot act upon it. If he can cross this one limitation, we can do such miraculous things that the world will have to dismiss our lives as a fairy tale. It can become like that if only we can take away our individual person from our thought, our emotion, our activity, and our energy.

The individual identification has become so strong that it has completely dislocated the human being from his original nature, and he has stopped operating as life. If he operates as just life and life alone, his capabilities are immense and no longer limited to what is contained within his physical form, because he has access to everything. The whole *tantra* yoga is about this, about breaking the individual shell so that what you do does not happen as a petty individual, but happens as a whole.

From the time, when I was just seven or eight years till I was twelve or thirteen, this took such grip of me from within. I would go to school, come back and sit somewhere where I wouldn't be disturbed for a few hours, either on top of the terrace or on top of a tree where I was out of range and nobody could access me. Nobody could get to that point, they could only scream which I could not hear anyway, because I was just totally focused on building my own world.

I sat there and just built a whole world of my own, another world, in the minutest detail. It is very difficult for people to understand this. If I wanted to create a flower, I went cell by cell. You know how much time it would take to mentally create this flower? Like this, point by point, point by point, I created a whole world of my own. At that time, the rhinoceros used to be my favorite animal. I had plenty of them in the world that I created – small ones, big ones, friendly ones, nasty ones, various kinds of rhinoceros and many other kinds of animals. I just sat like this, unmoving for five or six hours, building it piece by piece, and it became so real for me, hundred percent real.

My cousin brother, who was about a year younger than me, was in the house at that time. He came from the village, and was not studying properly there. My father was supposed to be a very strict disciplinarian and educator – though he couldn't manage with me – so they thought the boy would study better with us. One day, I took him on a tour of my world and after that he became insane, he wanted to go there every day. If I didn't take him, he would cry and bawl, and my mother was asking me, "What did you do to this boy?" It became so very real for him.

This is an imagination. According to modern physics and neurosciences, the distinction between imagination and hallucination is very thin, but there is a distinction. The distinction is just this – you have imagination which is unconscious, not a conscious process. If you could do the same hallucination consciously and empower it with your energy, it can become reality.

What is hallucination, what is reality? If you want to make a distinction, the important or the negative aspect of hallucination is that it is going uncontrolled, it is not conscious. It can take you anywhere and destroy your life because you have no control over what you are imagining. That is the problem. It is not empowered by life energy, so it is taking you away from

Mind Is Your Business

reality. It is not establishing you into reality nor is it helping you to create another reality. It is just taking you away from reality – that is the danger of hallucination. If you could control your hallucination, if you can have only beautiful hallucinations, what is wrong with it? You could hallucinate all the time. But the problem is you are unable to control the hallucination, so it will go whichever way it goes. Today it will be wonderful, tomorrow it can take you into the dumps, and after some time it is totally out of control. That amounts to madness.

If your imagination has gone so berserk that you are unable to control the process – that is hallucination. If you are consciously imagining, that is just imagination. People are crediting themselves with vivid imagination when actually their imagination is just going berserk. Berserk imagination and consciously imagining is very different. Consciously imagining will greatly enhance the capabilities of your mind. Just look at an ant and mentally try to rebuild every part of the ant. Just see what it takes. It will take a lot. Such a tiny creature, it takes so much application just to rebuild that ant in your mind. Have you ever done that? Not with the ant, with anything? Just rebuild every bit of your little finger in your mind and see. It is a phenomenal effort and if this effort can be taken to a certain point, it can become a magnificent process by itself. It can empower a human being in such a tremendous way.

When you are doing spiritual practices, how to know whether you are hallucinating or whether it is real? If there is a doubt that you are hallucinating, it is better that the benefit of doubt is given to hallucination than to your experience, because if there is a genuine experience, some transformation will happen by itself. If it is hallucination it is anyway a waste of time. So if you are in doubt, it is better to simply see that you are hallucinating because once you start crediting hallucination as real, then you will have no control over it. It will just go wild.

"If you transcend the mind, you transcend the karmic bondage also, completely."

Questioner: Through the practice of yoga, how can one transcend the mind?

Sadhguru: The whole process of yoga is to transcend the limitations of the mind. As long as you are in the mind, you are ruled by the past, because mind is just an accumulation of the past. If you are looking at life only through the mind, then you will make your future just like the past, nothing more, nothing less. Isn't the world enough proof of that? It does not matter what opportunities come our way through science, technology and many other things, aren't we repeating the same historical scenes again and again?

If you take a closer look at your own life, you will see the same repetition happening, because as long as you are functioning only through the prism of the mind, you are functioning only with the old data. The past is carried only in your mind. Only because your mind is active, past exists. Suppose all your mind ceases right now, is your past here? There is no past here, only present. The reality is only present, but past exists through our minds. Or in other words, mind is *karma.* If you transcend the mind, you transcend the *karmic* bondage altogether, in one stroke. If you want to solve them one by one, it may take a million years. In the process of solving, you are also building new stock of *karma.*

Your old stock of *karma* is not the problem at all. You should learn how not to create new stock. That is the main thing. Old stock will wear out by itself; no big things need to be done about it. But the fundamental thing is you learn how not to create new stock. Then, leaving the old stock is very simple.

If you transcend the mind, you transcend the *karmic* bondage also, completely. You don't really have to work it out because when you are playing with your *karmas,* you are playing with the non-existent. It is a trap of the mind. The past does not exist, but you are dealing with the non-existent, going about as if it is a reality. That is the whole illusion. Mind is the basis of this. If you transcend the mind, you transcend everything in one stroke.

The whole effort of spiritual sciences has always been how to transcend the mind, how to look at life beyond the limitations of the mind. Many people have defined yoga in many different ways. People say, "If you become one with the universe, it is yoga." "If you attain to God, it is yoga." "If you go beyond yourself, it is yoga." "If you are no more subject to the laws of the physical, it is yoga." All these things are fine and fantastic definitions, there is nothing wrong with them, but in terms of your experience, you cannot relate to them. Krishna said, "If you drop your ego, it is yoga." It's very nice, but how to drop your ego? You don't know which is you, which is yoga, which is ego. How to drop it? Somebody said, "If you become one with God, you are in yoga." You don't know where you are. You don't know where God is. How to become one?

But Patanjali nailed it this way – "To rise above the modifications of your mind, when you cease your mind, when you cease to be a part of your mind, that is yoga." All the influences of the world are entering you only through the instrument of the mind. If you can rise beyond the influence of your mind in full awareness, then you are naturally one with everything. The separation – you and me, time and space – has come only because of the mind. It is a bondage of the mind. If you drop the mind, you have dropped time and space. There is no such thing as this and that. There is no such thing as here and there. There is no such thing as now and then. Everything is here and now.

If you rise above all the modifications and manifestations of the mind, then you can play with the mind whichever way you want. You can use your mind with devastating impact in your life, but if you are in it, you will never realize the nature of the mind.

To use a simple analogy, they say man has lived on this planet for 200,000 years. In these 200,000 years, man did not realize that the planet is round. He thought it was flat. A few people had the foresight, with their mathematical calculations, and thought it could be a curve, but this argument would have gone on forever. Even now – forget the nonsensical things that you have read in your text book – walk up and down on the ground and see. Is this world flat or round? In your experience it is flat. When did this problem really get settled? When man began to fly, he went to the moon and looked down from there, now it was absolutely clear. No question of argument anymore.

We could not even grasp the simple shape of the planet when we were on it. Only when we took off, we could see it clearly. The same goes for your mind and the nature of your existence. Only when you create a little distance between you and the mind, only when you create a little distance between you and the body, you perceive the nature of the body and the mind. Otherwise, it is all mixed up. You are not conducting the process of the body and of the mind; you have become the process.

Once you learn how not to use the mind and simply look at life, it is the ultimate game you can play, because the Ultimate becomes available to you only through that. Through the distortions of the mind, you cannot perceive anything.

Have you heard of the word "Buddha?" When I say "Buddha," you are always thinking of that particular man –

Gautama the Buddha. Gautama is not the only Buddha, there have been thousands of Buddhas on this planet, and there still are. His second name is not Buddha, he is Gautama Siddhartha. He became a Buddha.

What does it mean to become a Buddha? *"Bu"* means *"Buddhi,"* the intellect. One who is above his intellect is a Buddha. One who is in his intellect is a non-stop suffering human being. No matter what is happening, his anxieties, his fears, his nonsense, his confusion will never go away as long as he is in the intellect.

Have you noticed this? No matter how well you are placed, constantly the mind is struggling. You think everything is perfect, but you turn back and see, your anxieties and your fears are sitting right there behind you like your tail. It follows you wherever you go. You look at the sunrise and you forget about everything, but when you turn back and see, it is right there. If you were below the mind, you would not know this kind of suffering.

It is because people are unable to bear the torture of the mind that they have devised many ways in society to go below the mind. Excessive eating, alcohol, excessive indulgence in physical pleasures, these are ways to go below the mind. People use them and for a few moments they can forget the torture. You hit the bottle and sleep. For a few hours, your mind does not bother you anymore because you have gone below the mind. There is a great pleasure and it is so relaxing because suddenly, the tortures of your mind are not there. So you get deeply addicted to it. But there is no such thing as going back. If you go below the mind by using a chemical, life always catches up with you with more intensity after that is over; suffering intensifies.

The nature of the evolutionary process is such that this being which was below the mind has right now evolved into the mind.

If it wants to become free, it has to go above the mind. "Above the mind" means you are out of your mind. Sometimes, maybe for a few moments, you may notice this in meditation – you are sitting here, your mind seems to be happening somewhere far away. Once this distance is there, whatever the mind is saying is not a problem anymore. What can it say? It is only recycling what it has gathered in a million different ways.

Once you have this distance, your ability to use the mind is tremendously enhanced. So if somebody says, "you are out of your mind," don't feel insulted. It is the highest compliment. They are saying you are a Buddha. People usually understand "out of the mind" as madness. Madness is of the mind. As long as you are in the mind, you cannot escape the madness. You may either be in socially accepted levels of madness or you may cross that socially accepted level, but some level of madness is going on in everybody. If you are out of the mind, can you be mad? Only if you are out of the circus of your mind, you will be hundred percent free of madness.

Mind Is Your Business

Isha Kriya

Isha Kriya™ is a simple yet potent practice rooted in the timeless wisdom of the yogic sciences. "Isha" refers to that which is the source of creation; "kriya" literally means "internal action." The purpose of Isha Kriya is to help an individual get in touch with the source of his existence, to create life according to his own wish and vision.

Through Isha Kriya, a 12-minute practice, an individual can pursue immediate and ultimate wellbeing, experiencing success in the social sphere, while nourishing the inner longing for the deeper dimensions of life. Isha Kriya empowers an individual towards a stress-free way of being, and promotes enhanced clarity, heightened energy levels, and a state of peacefulness and joy. Daily practice of Isha Kriya brings health, dynamism and happiness. It is a powerful tool to cope with the hectic pace of modern life.

Isha Kriya requires no special physical agility or previous experience of yoga to practice. It integrates seamlessly into one's daily life, bringing the possibilities of a spiritual process – which were once available only to yogis and ascetics – to every human being in the comfort of their own home. Created by Sadhguru, it has the potential to transform the life of anyone who is willing to invest just a few minutes a day. The instructions for Isha Kriya are given below.

You can also watch the Isha Kriya instruction video at http://www.ishakriya.com

Preparation

Sit facing east in a cross-legged posture, with your spine comfortably erect.

Keep your hands upon your thighs, with your palms facing up.

With your face slightly upturned, eyes closed, keep a mild focus between

your eyebrows.

The Meditation

This meditation will happen in three stages:

Stage 1:

Inhale and exhale gently and slowly.

With each inhalation, mentally say to yourself: "I am not the body."

The inhalation should last for the whole duration of that thought. With each exhalation, mentally say to yourself: "I am not even the mind."

The exhalation should last for the whole duration of that thought.

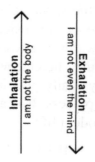

The breathing should be as shown in this diagram

Repeat this for 7 to 11 minutes.

Stage 2:

Utter a long "A" sound (as the "a" in father). The sound should come from just below the navel. You need not utter it very loud, but loud enough to feel the vibration.

Utter the long "A" sound 7 times, exhaling fully into each sound.

Mind Is Your Business

Stage 3:

Sit for 5 to 6 minutes with a slightly upturned face, and keep a mild focus between your eyebrows.

The total time of this practice is between 12 to 18 min. You can sit longer if you want.

PLEASE NOTE

While you sit for the Isha Kriya, do not pay attention to the activity of the mind or body. Whatever is happening in your body or your mind, just ignore it and simply sit there.

Do not take a break in between, as it will disturb the reorganization of energies that happens during the practice.

Each time you do the *kriya*, you must do it for a minimum of 12 minutes, and twice a day for 48 days (considered as a full mandala or cycle), or once a day for 90 days. The purpose of the *mandala* is to firmly establish the practice in your system. Thereafter, you can do it for a minimum of once a day.

Anyone can practice this *kriya* and enjoy its benefits. Simply follow the instructions without making any changes. This is a simple but very potent *kriya*.

You can remind yourself that – "I am not the body. I am not even the mind" – anytime during the day.

Questioner: What can I possibly gain out of this?

Sadhguru: Where is the need to meditate, first of all? Starting the process of life was not your conscious choice, it "happened" to you. When you were born your body was so small, and now it has grown. So obviously, the body is something that you gathered. It is an accumulation. What you call as "my body" is an accumulation of food. Similarly, what you call as "my mind" is an accumulation of impressions.

Whatever you accumulate can be yours, but it can never be you. The very fact you accumulated it means that you gathered it from somewhere else. Today you could gather a 70 kg body, but you can decide to make it a 60 kg body. You don't go looking for those 10 kgs, because they were an accumulation. Once you drop it, it is gone. Similarly, with your mind, it is an accumulation of impressions.

The moment you are identified in your experience, the moment you are identified with something that you are not, your perception goes completely haywire. You cannot perceive life the way it is; your perception is hugely distorted. So the moment you start experiencing this body, which you gathered from outside, as "myself," the moment you start experiencing the impressions that you have in your mind as "myself," you cannot perceive life the way it is. You will only perceive life the way it is necessary for your survival, and not the way it really is.

Yet once you have come as a human being, survival is very important, but it is not enough. If you had come here like any other creature on this planet, stomach full – life would be settled. But once you come here as a human being, life does not end with survival. Actually, for a human being, life begins only after survival is fulfilled.

So meditation gives you an experience and an inner state where "what is you" and "what is yours," is separated. There is a little distance, there is a little space between what is you and what you have accumulated. For now we can understand this as meditation.

What is the use of doing this? It brings an absolute clarity of perception. You see life just the way it is. No distortions about it; simply seeing life just the way it is. Right now if we see this very hall as a world, your ability to go through this world is only to the extent that you clearly see it. If I have no clarity of vision but if I have confidence and if I try to go through this, I'm going

Mind Is Your Business

to be a bumbling idiot. Whenever there is no perception, people try to overcome that by building confidence in them. Without the clarity of perception people are trying to make it up with other kinds of substitutes; there is no substitute for clarity.

Once you understand this you naturally become meditative; you want to clear up everything and just look at life the way it is, because you want to walk through life with least amount of friction, without stumbling on this or that.

Questioner: Why should my head be slightly upturned?

Sadhguru: Sitting with your head slightly upturned is not because you want to see something floating in the sky or imagine something. You keep your head upturned because when your system "looks" upward it becomes receptive. It is like opening a window. This is about becoming receptive to Grace. When you become willing and receptive, your body naturally arches up.

Questioner: What does this meditation do?

Sadhguru: This *kriya* will create a certain space between you and your body, between you and your mind. If at all there is any struggle in your life, it is because you identify yourself with these limited aspects of yourself.

So the essence of meditation is that it creates a space, a distance between you and what you refer to as your "mind." All the suffering you go through is manufactured in your mind, isn't it so? If you distance yourself from the mind, can there be suffering in you? This is the end of suffering.

Now while you are meditating, there is a distance between you and your mind, and you do feel peaceful. The problem is that the moment you open your eyes, you are again stuck with your mind.

If you meditate every day, a day will come when you open your eyes, and you can still experience that the mind is there and you are here. This is the end of suffering. When you are no longer identified with your body and mind, you will be in touch with the source of creation within you. Once this happens, Grace happens.

Whether you are here, or beyond, this is the end of suffering. That means your whole *karmic* bag – your past, or your unconscious mind – has been kept aside. It cannot have any influence over you. Once the past has no influence over you, then life becomes a huge potential. Every breath becomes such a tremendous possibility in your life, because the past is not playing any role in your existence here now. If you sit here, you are an absolute life. Life becomes effortless.

Questioner: What is the importance of the breath? Is there more to breathing well than being healthy?

Sadhguru: Breath is the thread which ties you to the body. If I take away your breath, your body will fall apart. It is the breath that has tied you to the body. What you call as your body and what you call as "me" have been tied together with breath. And this breath decides many aspects of who you are right now. For different levels of thought and emotion that you go through, your breath takes on different types of patterns. If you are angry you will be breathing one way. You are peaceful, you breathe another way. You are happy, you breathe another way. You are sad, you will breathe another way. Have you noticed this?

Based on this conversely is the science of *pranayama* and *kriya*: by consciously breathing in a particular way, the very way you think, feel, understand and experience life can be changed.

This breath can be used in so many ways as a tool to do other things with the body and the mind. You will see with the Isha Kriya, we are using a simple process of breath, but the

Mind Is Your Business

kriya itself is not in the breath. Breath is just a tool. Breath is an induction, but what happens is not about the breath.

Whichever way you breathe, that is the way you think. Whichever way you think, that is the way you breathe. Your whole life, your whole unconscious mind is written into your breath. If you just read your breath, your past, present and future is written there, in the way you breathe.

Once you realize this, life becomes very different. It needs to be known experientially; it is not something you can propound like this. If you know the bliss of simply sitting here, the blissfulness of just being able to simply sit here, not think anything, not do anything, simply sit here, just being life, then life would be very different.

In a way, what this means is today there is a scientific proof that without taking a drop of alcohol, without taking any substance, you can simply sit here and get drugged or stoned or drunk by yourself. If you are aware in a certain way, you can activate the system in such a way that if you sit here it is an enormous pleasure. Once simply sitting and breathing is such a great pleasure, you will become very genial, flexible, and wonderful because all the time you are in a great state within yourself. No hangover. Mind becomes sharper than ever before.

Questioner: What effect does uttering the sound "Aaa" have on me?

Sadhguru: When you utter the sound "Aaa," the maintenance center in your body gets activated. This is *Manipuraka* chakra, or the navel center. *Manipuraka* is just three-fourths of an inch below your navel. When you were in your mother's womb, the "maintenance" pipe was connected there. Now the tube is gone, but the maintenance center is still in your navel.

Now as there is a physical body, there is a whole energy body that we generally refer to as either *prana* or *shakti*. This energy, or *prana,* flows through the body in certain established patterns; it is not moving randomly. There are 72,000 different ways in which it moves. In other words, there are 72,000 pathways in the system through which it is flowing. So *nadis* are pathways or channels in the system. They do not have a physical manifestation; if you cut the body and look inside, you will not find these *nadis*. But as you become more and more aware, you will notice the energy is not moving at random, it is moving in the established pathways.

When you utter the sound "Aaa," you will see the reverberation will start about three-fourths of an inch below the navel and spread right across the body. Sound "Aaa" is the only reverberation which spreads right across the body because this is the only place where the 72,000 *nadis* meet and redistribute themselves. They all meet at *Manipuraka* and redistribute themselves. This is the only point in the body like that. If you utter the sound "Aaa," the reverberations of this sound are carried right across the system.

This reverberation can assist greatly in energizing your maintenance center. Activating this center will bring health, dynamism, prosperity and wellbeing.